Thaddeus Kosciusko Oglesby

**The Britannica answered and the South vindicated**

Thaddeus Kosciusko Oglesby

**The Britannica answered and the South vindicated**

ISBN/EAN: 9783337225223

Printed in Europe, USA, Canada, Australia, Japan

Cover: Foto ©ninafisch / pixelio.de

More available books at **www.hansebooks.com**

# THE BRITANNICA ANSWERED

AND

# THE SOUTH VINDICATED

— —

# A DEFENSE OF THE SOUTH

AGAINST THE ASPERSIONS

OF

# THE ENCYCLOPEDIA BRITANNICA

AND

# A CRITICISM OF THAT WORK

BY

T. K. OGLESBY.

MONTGOMERY, ALA:
PRESS OF THE ALABAMA PRINTING COMPANY.
1891.

# THE BRITANNICA ANSWERED,

# THE SOUTH VINDICATED.

## By T. K. OGLESBY.

[These pages comprise the articles published under the above heading in the Montgomery (Ala.,) *Advertiser*, January, 1891. They have been annotated and enlarged, and, in compliance with many requests—indicating what seems to be a very general desire—are now published in this form.]

—————

## I.

A communication in a late number of the *Advertiser* called attention to certain statements in the Encyclopedia Britannica, and asked if they could not be refuted. It referred to the statements in the Britannica's article on American Literature that "since the Revolution days the few thinkers of America born south of Mason and Dixon's line are outnumbered by those belonging to the single State of Massachusetts," and that "mainly by their connection with the north have Southern states been saved from sinking to the level of Mexico or the Antilles."

In refutation of these statements, reflecting so injuriously on the intellect and civilization of the South, I desire to lay before the public, through the widely read columns of the *Advertiser*, a summary of historical facts, showing that to the South, far more than to any other section, is this Union indebted for the genius, wisdom, enterprise, patriotism and valor that have given it so proud an eminence among the nations of the earth. The material for this purpose being too abundant to be comprised in a single article of appropriate length for the columns of a daily paper, this will, if you please, be followed by other articles in refutation of the Britannica's slur upon the South, and exposing its general worthlessness as a Cyclopedia for Americans, and especially for Southern people.

I will begin, then, the purposed refutation and exposure of the Britannica, with the following simple statement of historic facts:

The first President of the United States, and the most illustrious American—"the man first in war, first in peace, and first in the hearts of his countrymen," under whose leadership the colonies won their independence, and on whom, by common acclaim, is bestowed the title, "the father of his country,"—was a Southern man.

The first President of the Continental Congress was a Southern man,[1] and a Southern member of that Congress was the author and mover of the adoption of the resolution declaring the Colonies free and independent States.[2]

The greatest American orator—the man whose words most inspired the American heart and nerved the American arm in the struggle for independence—was a Southern man.

The author of the Declaration of Independence—the most famous production of an American pen—was a Southern man, and when the peoples of the United States met to celebrate the Centennial of that Declaration it was a Southern man who was selected to write the poem for the opening of that Centennial.[3]

"The father of the Constitution" was a Southern man;[4] its greatest expounder—the greatest American jurist—was a Southern man;[5] and when, in the fullness of time, the peoples of the Union came to celebrate the Centennial of that immortal instrument, it was a Southern man who was the chosen orator of that memorable and imposing occasion.[6]

For more than half the period of its existence the Government formed by that Constitution has been administered by Presidents who were Southern men, and the years of their administrations mark immeasurably the most splendid and prosperous eras of the Union. It was the statesmanship of a Southern President,[7] seconded by the ability of a Southern diplomat,[8] that extended the boundary of the United States from the Gulf of Mexico and the

1. Peyton Randolph.
2. Richard Henry Lee.
3. Sidney Lanier.
4. James Madison.
5. John Marshall.
6. Samuel F. Miller.
7. Jefferson.
8. James Monroe.

Mississippi river to the Pacific ocean on the northwest, thus adding to them a territory greater in extent than their original limits; it was Southern valor and Southern statesmanship that carried the boundary on the southwest from the Sabine to the Rio Grande, and added Texas, New Mexico and California to the United States—an addition of 20,000 square miles more than the original Thirteen States had; it was the prowess of a Southern soldier[1] that secured to the Republic all that territory northwest of the Ohio river, of which the States of Ohio, Indiana, Illinois, Michigan and Wisconsin were afterwards made; the policy that made that territory public domain—the common property of all the States—was the policy that has done more than any other to build up the Union, and it is indebted for that policy to the wisdom and patriotism of the Southern States of Maryland and Virginia,—to Maryland for proposing and urging it, and to Virginia for acceding to it, for that territory belonged to her, and in giving it to the United States for the sake of the Union she furnished the crowning proof of her devotion to that Union and became the "mother of States" as she was already the "mother of statesmen;" and the men who blazed the way for civilization in that vast region beyond the Mississippi and the Rocky Mountains —the most famous American explorers and adventurers—were Southern men.

For nearly two-thirds of the period of its existence has the Supreme Court of the United States—the sheet-anchor of the government—been presided over by Southern men, and their decisions constitute by far the wisest, purest and most luminous pages of the record of that august tribunal.

The writer of our national anthem was a Southern man;[2] the author of the Emancipation Proclamation was of Southern birth and lineage; and of the three contemporary American statesmen known as "the great trio,"[3] two were Southern men, and it was one of these two whose statesmanship and patriotism twice saved the Union from dismemberment.

The first shot in the second war of the United States with England was fired by a Southern man;[4] the most distinguished soldiers of that war were Southern men; the most complete and over-

1. George Rogers Clark.
2. Francis S. Key.
3. Clay, Calhoun and Webster.
4. Captain John Rodgers, of Maryland.

whelming defeat that any English army has ever experienced was
inflicted by Southern troops commanded by a Southern man;[1] the
man who performed what Admiral Nelson called "the most daring act of the age," and who received the thanks of all Europe
for overthrowing the Barbary powers and putting an end to their
inhuman cruelties, was a Southern man;[2] and the most distinguished soldiers of the war with Mexico were Southern men.

The first candidate of the Abolition party for the Presidency of
the United States was a Southern man;[3] so was its second candidate,[4] and so was its fourth and last and only elected candidate.

The first Sunday-School established in America was in a Southern State;[5] the first American to establish schools exclusively for
the education of young women was a Southern man;[6] the first female college in the world was established in a Southern State; [7]
the first post-graduate medical school in this country—the New
York polyclinic and hospital—was established by a Southern physician;[8] the first agricultural journal in this country was established by a Southern man;[9] and the first native Methodist itiner-
ant in America was a Southern man.[10]

The man who first gave a complete description of the Gulf
stream—who first marked out specific routes to be followed in
crossing the Atlantic—who first instituted the system of deep-sea
sounding—who first suggested the establishment of telegraphic
communication between the continents by cable on the bed of the
ocean, and who indicated the line along which the existing cable
was laid, was a Southern man;[11] and it was a Southern man who
originated the plan for splicing the cable in mid ocean.[12]

It was a Southern man who was declared by the French Acad-
emy of Sciences to have done more for the cause of agriculture
than any other living man;[13] a Southern man was the inventor of
the Gatling gun; the inventor of the machinery that first propelled
a boat by steam was a Southern man;[14] the first steamship that

1.  Andrew Jackson.
2.  Stephen Decatur.
3.  James G. Birney.
4.  John C. Fremont.
5.  At Savannah, Georgia.
6.  John Lyle, of Virginia.
7.  The Wesleyan Female College, Macon, Georgia.
8.  John A. Wyeth, of Alabama.
9.  "The American Farmer," by John S. Skinner, of Maryland.
10  William Watters, of Maryland and Virginia.
11.  Matthew F. Maury.
12.  Dr James C. Palmer, of Maryland.
13.  Cyrus H. McCormick.
14.  James Rumsey, of Maryland.

crossed the Atlantic went from a Southern city, whose name it bore and whose citizens had it built,[1] and its engine was constructed by a Southern man.[2] The inventor of the first comprehensive system of ciphers used by the Associated press,[3] and of the first pyrotechnic system of signals in the United States,[4] and the author of international fog-signals[5] —each of these was a Southern man.

That which has been pronounced the most original discovery ever made in physical science by an American was made by a Southern man;[6] the physician who first used sulphuric ether to produce anæsthesia for surgical operations,[7] the successful performer of the first operation for extirpation of the ovary on record —"the father of ovariotomy,"[8] the man distinguished as the greatest lithotomist of the nineteenth century,[9] and the world's greatest gynecologist,[10]—were all Southern men.

The most learned American mineralogist,[11] the greatest American naturalist,[12] the most famous American musician,[13] the artist known as the "American Titian,"[14] the greatest American architect,[15] and the world's greatest chess-player,[16] were all Southern men, as are the greatest American tragedian[17] and the most noted American dramatist,[18] and

### THE ONLY WOMAN ON RECORD

who was the wife of a governor, the sister of a governor, the niece of a governor, the mother of a governor, and the aunt and foster-mother of a governor, was a Southern woman.[19]

How stands the Britannica's assertion in the light of these facts?

1. Savannah.
2. Daniel Dod, of Virginia.
3. Alexander Jones, M. D., of North Carolina.
4. Henry J. Rogers, of Maryland.
5. Samuel P. Griffin, of Georgia.
6. The discovery of oxygen in the sun by photography, by Henry Draper, of Virginia.
7. Crawford W. Long, of Georgia.
8. Ephraim McDowell, of Virginia.
9. Benjamin W. Dudley, of Virginia.
10. J. Marion Sims, of South Carolina.
11. John Lawrence Smith, of South Carolina. He was employed by the Turkish government to explore its mineral resources, and it still derives part of its income from his discoveries. He received the order of Nichan Iftabar and that of the Medjidich from that government, and the order of St. Stanislas from Russia, and the cross of the Legion of Honor from Napoleon III. He was also inventor of the inverted microscope.
12. Audubon.
13. Gottschalk.
14. Allston.
15. Henry H. Richardson, of Louisiana.
16. Paul Morphy.
17. Edwin Booth.
18. Augustin Daly.
19. Mrs. Richard Manning, of South Carolina.

## II.

The facts I have already stated are enough and more than enough to vindicate the South from the aspersions of the Encyclopedia Britannica, but the occasion, and the fact that there are some who—unduly impressed by the high-sounding title and the imposing claims of that pretentious and ponderous collection of abstruse essays—are inclined to make a literary fetish of it, require that something further be here written in contrasting its statements with the truth of history.

The Britannica, in its article on American Literature, naming the two Carolinas as types of the Southern States, asserts that mainly by their connection with the North have they been saved from sinking to the level of Mexico or the Antilles—becoming, in short, a set of semi-barbarians. To this explicit assertion, so degrading to Southern people, I oppose an explicit denial, and I hale the Britannica before the tribunal of History, whose record it has falsified.

### A FURTHER APPEAL TO THE RECORD.

What says that record further? Was it in the South, or in the North—in the Carolinas, or in Massachusetts—that a law was made prescribing that a person, if once convicted of being a Quaker, should lose one ear,—if twice so convicted, should lose another ear,—and if convicted the third time of the diabolical crime of Quakerism, was to be bored through the tongue with a red-hot iron? Was it in the South, or in the North—in the Carolinas, or in Massachusetts—that a penalty was inflicted on any one who entertained a Quaker, and men and women were banished on pain of death and hung—for being Quakers? Was it in the South, or in the North—in the Carolinas, or in Massachusetts—that decrepit old men were hung and pressed to death—and pure, innocent women torn from their children and jailed and hung—as witches? Was it in the South, or in the North—in the Carolinas, or in Massachusetts—that children were tied neck and heels together till the blood was ready to gush from them, to make them swear falsely against their own mother—accused of being a witch? Was it here or there that men were hung for denying the existence of witchcraft? And were they of the North, or of the South—of

Massachusetts, or the Carolinas—the preachers and judges who
incited and applauded the jailing, and banishing, and torturing and
slaughtering of Quakers and "witches"?   To each and all of these
questions, History, with its inexorable, unerring pen, answers—
"Massachusetts!"

And where was it that, only a few years ago, the skin of persons
who had died as inmates of an alms-house was tanned and made
into articles of merchandise?   Have we not the authority of one
who is himself a distinguished citizen of that State for saying that
this tanning of human hide for commercial purposes was in Massachusetts?   Did not no less a personage than the governor of
that State say so?

### WORDS FROM WASHINGTON.

What was it that, most of all, filled the great heart of Washington with grief, and doubt, and despondency in that first winter of
the Revolution, when he was straining every nerve to keep an
army before Boston?   Read the answer in his own almost despair-
ing words.   Writing from Cambridge to a trusted friend—after
telling of the lack of powder and arms, and money—he says:
"These are evils but small in comparison of those which disturb
my present repose.   Our enlistments are at a stand.   The fears I
ever entertained are realized; that is, the discontented officers
have thrown such difficulties or stumbling-blocks in the way of
recruiting that I no longer entertain a hope of completing the
army by voluntary enlistments.   The reflection upon my situation
produces many an uneasy hour when all around me are wrapt in
sleep."   "To be plain," he continues, "these people are not to be
depended on;" and he advises appealing to their cupidity by the
offer of large bounties, for (he adds) "notwithstanding all the
public virtue which is ascribed to these people, there is no nation
under the sun that pays greater adoration to money than they do." [1]
Who were "these people"—the people of whom Washington
wrote those words?   Whence came the troops of whom Alexander
Graydon, a Revolutionary soldier of Pennsylvania, recorded in his
Memoirs these words:   "It appeared that the sordid spirit of gain
was the vital principle of this part of the army?" [2]   Were the peo-

---

1.  Washington to Joseph Reed.
2.  "I have been credibly informed that it was no unusual thing in the army before
Boston for a Colonel to make drummers and fifers of his sons, thereby not only being
able to form a very snug, economical mess, but to aid also considerably the revenue of
the family chest."  Graydon's Memoirs, p. 118.

ple of whom Washington wrote, and the troops to whom Graydon
referred, from the North, or from the South—from New England
or the Carolinas? Again, History, making response to this question, answers: "New England!" (Who can help thinking, right
here, in connection with the words of Washington and Graydon,
of that general of the Revolution whose "sordid spirit of gain"
made him a traitor to his country? Benedict Arnold was not a
Carolinian nor a Southern man.)

HELP FROM THE SOUTH.

With enlistments at a stand, and without powder for the troops
he had, and among a people "whose vital principle seemed to be
the sordid spirit of gain," what wonder is it that the unselfish
Southern patriot had such gloomy forebodings? Happily for him
and for the country his sorest immediate need was about to be sup-
plied. A British ship loaded with powder was captured off
Savannah about this time by a vessel commissioned for the purpose by the Provincial Congress of Georgia, and, badly as it was
needed at the South, a large portion of it was immediately dis-
patched to the army at Cambridge—for the South had declared
that "the cause of Boston is the cause of all." This was the first
capture ordered by any American Congress, the vessel that made
it was the first vessel commissioned for warfare in the Revolution,
and it was this powder, thus captured, that enabled Washington
to drive the British from Boston.

TALLEYRAND RELATES AN INCIDENT, AND CHANNING AND BRYANT

WRITE LETTERS.

Talleyrand relates that when he was in this country he met a
citizen of Maine who had never seen Washington. Talleyrand
asked him if he would not, when he visited Philadelphia, like to
see that great man. The Maine citizen said he would be pleased
to see Washington, but evinced a much greater desire "to see Mr.
Bingham, who they say is so rich." In the eyes of the Maine man
George Washington was "small potatoes" in comparison with "the
rich Mr. Bingham."

Nearly a quarter of a century after Washington penned at Cambridge the letters quoted above, William Ellery Channing wrote
from Richmond these words: "I blush for my own people when
I compare the selfish prudence of a Yankee with the generous con-

AND THE SOUTH VINDICATED.

fidence of a Virginian. There is one single trait which attaches me to the people here more than all the virtues of New England, —they love money less than we do; they are more disinterested; their patriotism is not tied to their purse strings." Still forty years later we find William Cullen Bryant, of Massachusetts, writing—"the South certainly has the advantage over us in the point of manners."

### THE TRAIL OF THE MONEY DEVIL OVER THEM ALL.

The Vice-President of the United States who accepted bribes and perjured himself to escape exposure—the Speaker of the House of Representatives (afterwards the candidate of the Republican party for the Presidency) who gave the influence of his high place in exchange for lucre—the Cabinet Minister who was impeached for selling appointments to the highest bidder—and the Credit Mobilier Congressmen—were these of the North or the South? All, all Northern.

### THE BRITANNICA SAYS IT WAS.

Was it their connection with the people whose manners Bryant characterized as being inferior—whose "patriotism" (said Channing) "is tied to their purse-strings"—whose "vital principle" (said Graydon) "appeared to be the sordid spirit of gain"—who (said Washington) "pay greater adoration to money than any nation under the sun, and are not to be depended on"—was it by their connection with these people and their Quaker-hanging, "witch"-killing ancestry and bribe-taking posterity that Southern people have been saved from sinking into barbarism? The Britannica says it was. What says the truth of history?

### THE MEN HE DID DEPEND ON.

"These people are not to be depended on," wrote Washington of the New England troops, but at a later period, when he was sending reinforcements to General Gates in response to an appeal from that officer, he wrote: "I have despatched Col. Morgan with his corps of riflemen to your assistance. This corps I have great dependence on." Later, when he himself needed reinforcements and asked that Morgan and his men be sent back, Gates replied that he could not then afford "to part with the corps the army of General Burgoyne was most afraid of." History tells us that the men on whom Washington had such "great dependence,"

and of whom Burgoyne's army "was most afraid" were—not from
New England, but—from Virginia, that land where, said Channing, "their patriotism is not tied to their purse-strings."

### THREE HISTORIC DOCUMENTS.

In the archives of the Government at Washington are three
historic documents worthy of consideration in this connection.
The first one, in point of time, reads thus:

"Headquarters Army of Northern Virginia.

### "CHAMBERSBURG, PA., June 27, 1863.

General Order No. 73.

"The Commanding General has observed with marked satisfac-
tion the conduct of the troops on the march, and confidently an-
ticipates results commensurate with the high spirit they have
manifested.   No troops could have displayed greater fortitude or
better performed the arduous marches of the past ten days.   Their
conduct in other respects has, with few exceptions, been in keeping with their character as soldiers, and entitles them to approba-
tion and praise.   There have, however, been instances of forget-
fulness on the part of some that they have in keeping the yet un-
sullied reputation of the army, and that the duties exacted of us
by civilization and Christianity are not less obligatory in the
country of our enemy than in our own.   The Commanding General considers that no greater disgrace could befall the army, and
through it our whole people, than the perpetration of the barbarous outrages upon the innocent and defenceless, and the wanton
destruction of private property that have marked the course of the
enemy in our own country.   Such proceedings not only disgrace
the perpetrators and all connected with them, but are subversive
of the discipline and efficiency of the army, and destructive of
the ends of our present movements.   It must be remembered that
we make war only on armed men, and that we can not take vengeance for the wrongs our people have suffered without lowering
ourselves in the eyes of all whose abhorrence has been excited by
the atrocities of our enemy, and offending against Him to whom
vengeance belongeth.

"The Commanding General therefore earnestly exhorts the
troops to abstain, with most scrupulous care, from unnecessary or
wanton injury to private property, and he enjoins upon all officers

to arrest and bring to summary punishment all who shall in any way offend against the orders on this subject.

[Signed.]                  "R. E. LEE, General."

The second one of the documents referred to is a letter dated —"Headquarters of the Army, Washington, December 18, 1864," addressed to "Major-General W. T. Sherman, Savannah," and concluding thus: "Should you capture Charleston, I hope that by some accident the place may be destroyed, and if a little salt should be sown upon its site, it may prevent the growth of future crops of nullification and secession.

[Signed.]            "Yours truly,

               "H. W. HALLECK, Chief-of-Staff."

The third document is a letter in which are these words: "I will bear in mind your hint as to Charleston, and do not think 'salt' will be necessary. When I move, the Fifteenth Corps will be on the right of the right wing, and their position will naturally bring them into Charleston first ; and, if you have watched the history of that corps, you will have remarked that they generally do their work pretty well. The truth is, the whole army is burning with an insatiable desire to wreak vengeance upon South Carolina. I almost tremble at her fate, but feel that she deserves all that seems in store for her.   *   *   *    We must make old and young, rich and poor, feel the hard hand of war as well as their organized armies." This letter is dated—"Headquarters Military Division of the Mississippi, in the Field, Savannah, December 24, 1864;" is addressed to "Major-General H. W. Halleck, Chief-of-Staff, Washington, D. C.," and is signed—"W. T. Sherman, Major-General."

The burning dwelling houses along the line of his march, and the wail of women and children left starving and unsheltered in the depth of winter attested how well "the Fifteenth Corps" maintained the reputation to which their commander so proudly pointed.[1]

### WHICH WAS THE BARBARIAN?

Which was the barbarian,—the Southerner, who wrote the first of these documents, or the Northern man who wrote the last? The Southerner, from a long line of Southern ancestry; or the Northern man, with generations of Northern ancestors behind him? Robert E. Lee, or William Tecumseh Sherman?

1. See Addendum A.

## III.

The Britannica is particularly at fault in citing the Carolinas as types of the Southern States in its assertion (in the article on American Literature) that they have been saved from sinking to the level of Mexico or the Antilles mainly by their connection with the North. A more unfortunate reference, to illustrate its imputation of Southern barbarism, could not have been made by the foreign cyclopedia, as will, I think, be clearly shown by what I will here say in relation to the stigma it puts upon those two States especially, and through them on the South generally.

And first, of

### THE OLD NORTH STATE.

There are no people in the Union nor in the world among whom are to be found more of the attributes of sound mental, moral, and physical manhood than those which characterize the people of North Carolina. Her sons shed, at Alamance, the first blood spilled in the Colonies in resistance to British rule—long before a gun was fired at Lexington and Concord ; her Mecklenburg County—which Cornwallis called a "hornet's nest," and where he encountered, he said, the most obstinate rebels he had found in America—proclaimed its "declaration of independence" more than a year before the one at Philadelphia; she was the first Colony to act as a unit in favor of independence; and about the time a deputation of Bostonians were appealing to Washington to allow the beleaguered British to get out of Boston unmolested, for fear of disturbing trade and damaging the shops by a fight, North Carolina soldiers, at Moore's Creek Bridge, were winning the first real victory on a battle field of the Revolution.

### A STRIKING COINCIDENCE.

The Bostonians above-mentioned were undoubtedly the ancestry of those other representative citizens of Massachusetts who, about forty-years later, were secretly plotting in a convention at Hartford the secession of the New England States from the Union, because their trade was hurt by the war for the maintenance of American rights and honor which was then going on between the United States and England, and the Hartford Conventionists were unquestionably the close kith and kin of those other representative citizens of New England who, during that trying time in the history of our country, burned blue lights on the Connecticut coast to put the British on guard against Decatur's plans for attacking them ; and it is a striking coincidence that just about the time when New England was thus, by threats of secession, endeavoring to paralyze the arm of the Government and giving aid and comfort to the enemy in time of war, descendants of the above-mentioned North Carolinians were mauling the life out of that enemy at New Orleans.

Who can doubt that Decatur, the Southerner and the patriot, had the secession plotters and blue-light burners of New England in his mind when he uttered the memorable sentiment: "Our country! In her intercourse with foreign nations, may she always be in the right. But our country, right or wrong"?

### THE FIRST SECESSION CONVENTION.

That Convention at Hartford was the first Secession Convention in the history of the Union, and was presided over by the great-grand-father of Mr. Henry Cabot Lodge, of Force Bill notoriety, who is now a representative of Massachusetts in Congress; and it was just about four years before the holding of that Convention that Josiah Quincy, also of Massachusetts, made the first speech in Congress in favor of secession. Thus does the record show that while the South was fighting to uphold the rights and honor of the Union, the New England States, with "their patriotism tied to their purse-strings," were plotting to break it up because the war interrupted their trade for awhile.

### ANOTHER COINCIDENCE.

To return to the Revolution. About the time when Arnold, the New England general who turned traitor for British gold, was plundering in Virginia, North Carolinians, under Sevier and Shelby, Cleveland and McDowell, were striking the British that deadly blow at King's Mountain that turned the tide of the Revolution and eventuated in the capture of Cornwallis and his army at Yorktown, and in the independence of all the Colonies and the establishment of the United States of America.

### THE BRITANNICA DOESN'T MENTION THEM.

But Sevier, and Shelby, and King's Mountain are names not to be found in the Britannica's history of the United States. A history

of the United States with no allusion to the battle of King's
Mountain! Think of a history of France without any account of
Valmy! Or a history of Germany without the story of the battle
which rolled back from that country the Roman invasion and
caused the Roman Emperor to cry in vain to Varus for his legions!
For, but for King's Mountain the British monarch would not have
had to mourn his legions lost at Yorktown.

In this connection it may be noted that the Britannica has no
article on Yorktown, and its article on Saratoga makes no mention of the capture of Burgoyne's army there—the very thing that
gives Saratoga its historic interest.

Cornelius Harnett, Richard Caswell, Robert Howe—glorious
names in American history,—James Iredell, as able a jurist as ever
sat on the bench of the Supreme Court of the United States;
William Gaston, Willie P. Mangum, George E. Badger,—all these
have shed luster on the American name, in the field or in the
forum, and all were of North Carolina, but not one of them is
named in the Britannica.

And that most illustrious son of "the Old North State"—
the real American Cincinnatus—whom Jefferson called "the last
of the Romans," and of whom John Randolph said—"He is the
wisest, the purest, the best man I ever knew;" what of him in the
Britannica? Search it through and you will never learn from its
diffuse pages that such a man as Nathaniel Macon ever lived,—a
man of whom it is recorded that during fifty-seven years of political life and power he never recommended any of his family to
public office. (What a contrast to another public functionary, of
later years—a President of the United States and a Northern
man, of whom it was said that he quartered on the public treasury
all his own relatives, all his wife's relatives, and all the relatives
of these relatives, to the remotest cousinhood.) No, you will find
nothing of Nathaniel Macon in the Britannica, but you will find
in it over a column about one Ambrosius Theodosius Macrobius,
who died more than a thousand years ago.

James K. Polk, eleventh President of the United States, was a
North Carolinian, and Bancroft, the great American historian, has
said that, "viewed from the standpoint of results, Polk's was perhaps the greatest administration in our national history, certainly
one of the greatest."

## AND THE BIGGEST MAN!

Finally, Nature, as if not satisfied with bestowing so many other marks of distinction upon North Carolina, brought into being and reared upon her soil the biggest man, in mere physical proportions, of whom there is any mention in the history of this country.[1]

## SOUTH CAROLINA.

And South Carolina—"the nurse of manly sentiment and heroic enterprise," where has ever been found in the highest degree "that sensibility of principle, that chastity of honor which feels a stain like a wound and inspires courage while it mitigates ferocity;" South Carolina—where life's most exquisite grace abides—saved from barbarism by connection with Massachusetts! Shades of the long line of statesmen, heroes, orators and scholars of the Palmetto State who have illumined history's pages by your words and deeds, could ignorance or reckless misrepresentation further go?

It was William Henry Drayton, of South Carolina, whose writings contributed so much to enlighten the public mind in this country and Great Britain during the Revolutionary period, and to whose celebrated charge to the Charleston grand jury Mr. Jefferson has been thought to have been indebted for some of the most effective parts of the Declaration of Independence; it was John Rutledge, of South Carolina, whose services were of such inestimable value to the American cause in its most desperate straits,—who was pronounced by Patrick Henry to be the greatest orator in the Continental Congress,—who was the first associate justice of the Supreme Court of the United States and the second Chief Justice appointed by Washington; it was John Laurens, of South Carolina, who was distinguished as "the Chevalier Bayard of the Revolution," and who was said by John Adams to have done more for the United States in the short time of his being in Europe as their special envoy than all the rest of their diplomatic corps put together; it was Francis Marion who was the most capable and famous partisan soldier of the Revolution; it was Charles Cotesworth Pinckney, of South Carolina, who was the author of the clause in the Constitution forbidding the requiring of any religious test as a qualification for office or public trust in the United States.

1. Miles Darden. He weighed over 1,000 pounds.

## DID THEY GET THEM FROM THE NORTH?

Did Laurens get the knightly spirit of a Bayard from connection in any way with the ancestry who transmitted the qualities that inspired William T. Sherman when he wrote that he didn't think it would be necessary to sow salt on the site of Charleston when "the Fifteenth Corps" got in their work on that city? Did Pinckney get his enlightened and statesman-like principles of religious toleration from the teaching and example of the Massachusetts preachers and judges and people who tortured and hung Quakers and "witches" and drove Roger Williams, the Baptist, into the wilderness among the savages, for maintaining that man is responsible to God alone in matters of conscience, and that no human power has the right to intermeddle in them?[1]

### MORE HISTORIC NAMES NOT IN THE BRITANNICA.

It was William J. Lowndes, a South Carolinian, whom the Duke of Argyll and Mr. Roscoe pronounced the wisest young man they had ever met, and who was declared by Henry Clay to be the wisest man he had ever known in Congress; and yet you might read every word in the Britannica without learning that such a man as William J. Lowndes ever lived.[2] It was Langdon Cheves, of South Carolina, statesman, jurist, and financier, from whom Washington Irving said he had for the first time an idea of the manner in which the great Greek and Roman orators must have spoken, but no word of Cheves do you find in the Britannica. It gives space enough to the fights at Lexington and Concord and Bunker Hill, but dismisses with one line the disastrous defeat of the British at Charleston by Moultrie and the brave Carolinians under him, and makes no mention of that distinguished soldier nor of William Jasper, one of the most famous of American heroes, for whom counties and towns have been named all over the land, and to whose memory bronze and marble monuments have been reared. Nor can you find anything in it of Gadsden; nor Pick-

1. See Addendum B.
2. In an address on the Fourteenth Congress, Richard Henry Wilde, himself a member of that body, alluded to Mr. Lowndes in the following language: "Pre-eminent among the members of the Fourteenth Congress was a gentleman of South Carolina, now no more, the purest, the calmest, the most philosophical of our country's modern statesmen; one, no less remarkable for gentleness of manners and kindness of heart, than for that passionless, unclouded intellect, which rendered him deserving of the praise, if man ever deserved it, of merely standing by and letting reason argue for him; the true patriot, incapable of selfish ambition, who shunned office and distinction, yet served his country faithfully, because he loved her. He, I mean, who consecrated by his example, the noble precept, so entirely his own, that the first station in a Republic was neither to be sought after or declined; a sentiment so just and so happily expressed that it continues to be repeated because it cannot be improved."

ens; nor Legare, the distinguished scholar; nor Preston, the famous orator; nor Petigru, the great lawyer; nor Sims, the great physician, who began in Alabama that career which brought him world-wide fame, and honors from the crowned heads of Europe.

### AN EXCELLENT WORK FOR ANTIQUARIANS.

It tells us nothing of McDuffie, the statesman and splendid orator, but it gives half a column to one Maudonius, a deacon who lived in Constantinople about 1,500 years ago; it gives four lines in fine print in an obscure foot-note to Rutledge, the patriot, statesman, orator and jurist, who was such a potent factor in determining the destiny of this great country, and over two columns in big print to Claudius Namatianus Rutilius, who appears to have written a Latin poem about 1,500 years ago; it says nothing of Edmund Pendleton, of Virginia,—said by Jefferson to have been the ablest man in debate he ever met, but it devotes over three columns to a painter named Pinturicchio, who lived before Columbus discovered America; and it gives so much space to an English poet named Drayton, who lived some hundreds of years ago, that it has no room for any mention whatever of the celebrated Carolina patriot, statesman and jurist of that name.

It is not to be denied that the Britannica is an excellent work for antiquarians.

## IV.

What sort of Cyclopedia for Americans is it that finds plenty of room for telling about an English comedy writer named Randolph, who lived about three hundred years ago, but no room at all for such statesmen as Peyton Randolph and Edmund Randolph; nor for George Wythe, the eminent jurist, "the honor of his own and the model of future times;" nor for any one of the Tuckers, that family of scholars, statesmen, jurists and soldiers; nor for Cary, the intrepid patriot; nor for Giles, the accomplished debater and parliamentary tactician; nor for Henry Lee, soldier, orator, statesman,—the "Light-Horse Harry" of the Revolution, and father of the immortal Robert E. Lee? That is just the kind of Cyclopedia the Britannica is. It finds room for but two of all of the illustrious family of Lee, but you would never know, from its sketch of Richard Henry Lee, that he was ever President of the Continental Congress of America.

Upon what principle of cyclopedia-making did the authors of the Britannica proceed when they gave an article over a column long to "Harvard" College and none at all to "William and Mary," the college that gave Washington his first commission and public employment and the opportunity for developing his genius, —that claims for her children five of the seven signers of the Declaration of Independence from Virginia,—the college among whose children were "Jefferson, the author of the Declaration, and Wythe, his preceptor; Peyton Randolph, too, the president of the First Congress, and Edmund Randolph, the first Attorney General and Secretary of State and one of the wisest of the framers of our Constitution; and James Monroe, President of the United States; then John Marshall, the great Chief Justice; John Tyler, Federal judge, Governor of Virginia (and father of another of her worthy sons, President Tyler), who instituted the first measures for the convention to frame our Constitution in place of that of the Confederation; John Taylor, of Caroline; the Blands, the Pages, the Nicholases, the Burwells, the Grymeses, the Lewises, the Lyons, the Mercers, the Cockes, the Bollings, the Nicholsons, and Carringtons, and a long list of others almost as eminent, and quite as worthy, whose names are 'familiar in our mouths as house-

hold words,' were of the number she had trained for the service of
the country prior to the Revolution, to say nothing of the hosts of
others since that time, trained in her sacred groves, who went
from her to impress themselves on the society and institutions of
the land, as grave and worthy judges, eloquent and able advo-
cates, brave warriors on land and sea, faithful and honorable men
in every station"?[1]  Well has it been said of "William and Mary,"
by the same distinguished speaker whom I have just quoted,
that "the influence of her sons sent out since the Revolution and
before the late war, on the society and institutions of our country,
would alone establish her claims as one of the most glorious, successful, and beneficent of the colleges of America."

But "William and Mary," the patron of Washington, the Alma
Mater of Jefferson, and the Randolphs, and Monroe, and Mar-
shall, is not deemed worthy of an article in the Encyclopedia
Britannica.

When an intelligent American sees the number and sort of foreign subjects to which the Britannica devotes so much space, how
can he help being astonished on finding in it no articles on such
historic characters as Francis Asbury—the first bishop of the
Methodist Episcopal Church ordained in the United States, to
whose labors, more than to any other human cause, Methodism in
America owes its excellent organization and wonderful growth;
and Thomas Coke; and Jesse Lee, of Virginia—whose labors in
New England earned him the title of the "Apostle of Methodism;"
and James O. Andrew—on whose social relations began the division of the Methodist Episcopal Church in America; and Joshua
Soule—that man of giant intellect and heroic mould, the senior
bishop of the Methodist Episcopal Church South; and Samuel
Harris—the "apostle of Virginia," a name to be held in everlasting
remembrance by the Baptist brotherhood; and Samuel Davies—
founder of the Presbyterian Church in Virginia; and Moses
Stuart—the father of biblical learning in America; and John
Carroll—the ardent and powerful friend of American liberty and
the first bishop of the Roman Catholic Church in the United
States; and Archbishop Hughes—that courageous and powerful
champion of his church; and Bishop England—name especially
dear to the people of Charleston and South Carolina; and Alexan-

1. Address of Henry C. Semple to the Society of the Alumni of William and Mary
College, July 4th, 1890.

der Campbell, founder of the church of "The Disciples of Christ"? These were colossal figures in the religious life of America, but not an article on any one of them is to be found in the Britannica. But it gives us swarms of English and other foreign preachers and small theologians.

### JOHN WESLEY.

Two statements of the Britannica are so remarkable for their display of ignorance and narrow prejudice as to deserve a paragraph to themselves right here. They are, first, that "John Wesley was not the author of any original hymns," and, second, that "Wesley has no claims to rank as a thinker, or even as a theologian"! That is what the Britannica says of the man of whom Macaulay wrote: "He was a man whose eloquent and logical acuteness might have rendered him eminent in literature; whose genius for government was not inferior to that of Richelieu"!

### ON THE WRONG SIDE OF THE LINE.

Why has the Britannica omitted from its pages the names of such distinguished Americans as William R. King, conspicuous for nearly fifty years in the public life of this country, as representative and senator in congress, foreign minister and vice-president; and Hugh L. White, whose name is so intimately and honorably associated with many of the most memorable events of American history; and John M. Berrien, "the Cicero of the American senate;" and William C. Rives, senator and foreign minister and author; and John Forsyth, senator, foreign minister and secretary of state;[1] and William Wirt, so distinguished as lawyer, orator, and man of letters—for twelve years Attorney-General of the United States; and William Pinkney, the great lawyer and orator, who was cabinet officer, foreign minister and senator; and Stephen Decatur, the most celebrated commander of his time in the American navy, whose daring and efficiency challenged the attention and admiration of the civilized world, and whose tragic and untimely death plunged this whole country into mourning? The fame of these men is co-extensive with the Republic, but not an article on one of them is to be found in the Britannica! Two of them were born in that very North Carolina to which the

---

1. By his genius, culture, courteous deportment, and his unrivalled eloquence, even from young manhood he was a favorite of the people, and became the most brilliant light of Jackson's administration. It is probable that the State (Georgia) never had a man so variously gifted as Forsyth.—*Richard Malcolm Johnston.*

Britannica specially points in proof of its charge of the barbarism of the South. Why are they all left out of the Britannica's biographical department? Is it because they did not hail from Massachusetts—that State whose "thinkers," says the Britannica, "outnumber all those born south of Mason and Dixon's line since the Revolution"—that State, connection with which has saved the South "from sinking to the level of Mexico or the Antilles"?

If the author of that unrivaled lyric, "My Life is like the Summer Rose," had dwelt in Massachusetts, the Britannica would doubtless have contained a notice of him, but as he lived in that barbarous region south of Mason and Dixon's line, the Britannica knows not of him. Yet Richard Henry Wilde was eminent as lawyer, orator and statesman, as well as poet. On Zachary Taylor it has seventeen lines, but of "Tape-Worms" it has thirteen solid columns, and on "Trematoda" it is full and thrilling in the extreme, as, for instance, where it tells us that "all Trematoda have been commonly regarded as devoid of a body-cavity, and as consisting of parenchymatous tissue, but that recent researches show that the intercellular spaces in this tissue are to be regarded as the homologue of a cœlom." This is highly important if true, as the papers used to say of news from the front during the war, and the clear, intelligible language in which it is expressed cannot fail of appreciation by any person rejoicing in the possession of the Britannica. It manages to publish seven columns on Texas without ever telling what city is the capital of the State, and without any allusion to Moses and Stephen F. Austin, or to the Alamo, that American Thermopylæ, where Bowie, and Crockett, and Travis, and their comrades met death and covered themselves and the American name with undying glory. If the Alamo had been on Massachusetts or English soil, would it have been thus totally ignored by the Britannica? Rather, in that case, would not a few "Tape-Worms" and "Trematoda" have been sacrified, if necessary, to make room for some notice of the hundred and fifty heroes who for ten days held four thousand foemen at bay, and, like the Old Guard at Waterloo, died at last but never surrendered? Room is found in the Britannica for a special and separate article on "Concord" and the small skirmish that occurred there with little loss of life; but no such room for the Alamo and its devoted band of immortals; nor for King's Mountain; nor

Guilford Court-house; nor Yorktown, memorable for two sieges, the first of which resulted in the capture of an entire British army and the achievement of American independence, and the last of which occurred during the late war between the States, when the Confederate army was besieged there by the Union army. In such a complete, all-round, all-over-the-world, lay-over-everything cyclopedia as the Britannica claims to be, shouldn't Yorktown have at least as prominent a place as Concord?

But I was forgetting that Yorktown, and Guilford Court-House, and King's Mountain, and the Alamo, like William and Mary College, are on the Britannica's barbarous side of Mason and Dixon's line; while Concord,—Concord is in Massachusetts, the Britannica's favorite spot of American earth.

It has nothing at all about—but why go on with the long list of historic names and places of the South of which the Britannica takes no note? Neither time nor space will permit it here, for their name is legion. Has not enough been said to show its amazing and culpable deficiency in this respect?

## V.

Is it necessary to add, in further proof of the Britannica's animus towards the South, that, though it finds no place in its twenty-four huge volumes for William R. King or William L. Yancey, it gives ample room to John Brown and William Lloyd Garrison? That it puts Webster, Seward and Sumner down as "statesmen," and Calhoun and Clay as "politicians," merely? That, while it has no article on Jefferson Davis, it finds occasion to allude disparagingly to him? That it has no article on the Confederate States, but alludes to them incidentally in the article purporting to be a history of the United States, and, among many other misstatements, says that there were 700,000 soldiers in the Confederate armies at the beginning of 1863 (while the truth is, they did not have that many during the whole period of the war)? That it says that where the whites of the Southern States failed to gain political control by bribery and threats, they resorted to whipping and arson and murder? It does indeed say these things, and much more in the same vein; and discriminates against the South in its biographies in the manner stated, all of which no doubt greatly delights the Hoars and the Lodges, the Shermans and the Chandlers, and those of their ilk, who are so fond of describing the South as still being in the twilight of civilization—still a land of semi-barbarous people. They can quote, you see, the Encyclopedia Britannica to prove the justness of their description. The Britannica is a very popular book in Massachusetts.

### ITS EXPOSITION OF THE CONSTITUTION.

The person who goes to the Encyclopedia Britannica for instruction as to the nature of the Government of the United States will receive a totally erroneous impression concerning it. He will read there the dogmatic assertion that "it was the people of the whole United States" (that is, in the aggregate,) "that established the Constitution." This, of course, is a wholly untrue and altogether absurd assertion, directly in conflict with indisputable public records, and plainly disproved by the last clause of the Constitution itself, in these words: "The ratification of the conventions of nine States shall be sufficient for the establishment of this Constitution between the States so ratifying the same." "If this were a consolidated government," said Henry Lee in the Virginia Convention that was considering the question of ratifying the Constitution,—"If this were a consolidated government, ought it not to be ratified by a majority of the people as individuals, and not as States? Suppose Virginia, Connecticut, Massachusetts and Pennsylvania had ratified it; these four States, being a majority of the people of America, would, by their adoption, have made it binding on all the States, had this been a consolidated government."

As it neither was nor could have been established by a majority vote of the people of the whole United States, so neither can it be changed by a majority vote of the people. As it could be established only by the votes of nine of the original thirteen States, acting as States in convention assembled, so neither can it be changed unless three-fourths of the States, through their legislatures or conventions, consent that it shall be changed. No mere majority vote, either of the people or of the States, established or could have established the Constitution. Without the approval and ratification of nine of the thirteen States, it would have been of no more consequence than the paper on which it was written. No mere majority vote, either of the people or of the States, can change or amend it. A proposed amendment must be approved and ratified by three-fourths of the States in the manner above named before it is of any more consequence than the paper on which it is written.

THE BRITANNICA VERSUS JEFFERSON DAVIS, ALEXANDER H. STE-
PHENS, AND JAMES MADISON.

If the Britannica's statement were true, the votes of a majority of the people in the thirteen States would have established the Constitution over all. But against that statement let me oppose the words of Jefferson Davis, an American statesman and historian. Mr. Davis says: "The Constitution was never submitted to the people of the United States in the aggregate, or as a people. No such political community as the people of the United States exists or ever did exist. There has never been any such thing as a vote of 'the people of the United States in the aggregate;' no such people is recognized by the Constitution; no such political community has ever existed. * * * The monstrous fiction that they acted as one people 'in their aggregate capacity' has not an atom of fact to serve as a basis." (Rise and Fall of the Confederate Government, vol. 1, chapters 2, 3, and 4.)

Alexander H. Stephens, another American statesman and historian, says: "The Constitution was submitted to the States for their approval and ratification, and not to the people of the whole country, in the aggregate, and it was agreed to and ratified by the States as States, and not by the people of all the States in one aggregate mass." (The War Between the States, vol. 1, Col. 4.)

James Madison was the fourth President of the United States, and is called "the father of the Constitution" from the fact that it is more his work than that of any other one man. Writing of it prior to its adoption by the number of States necessary to establish it, he said: "That the ratification of the Constitution will be a federal and not a national act is obvious from this single consideration, that it is to result neither from the decision of a majority of the people of the Union nor from that of a majority of the States. It must result from the unanimous assent of the several States that are parties to it." (The Federalist, xxxix.)

Now, where is the truth concerning the Constitution and the nature of this Government most likely to be found,—in the British Cyclopedia, or in the writings of such American statesmen as Davis, Stephens and Madison?

## THIS IS NOT A GOVERNMENT OF A MAJORITY OF THE WHOLE PEOPLE.

The Britannica abounds in statements as misleading as the one just so overwhelmingly refuted, the pernicious purport of them all being that this is a national government instead of a "federal" one, as Mr. Madison called it;—that it is a government of the people of this country as one nation instead of a federation of States;— that it is a government formed and ruled by the vote of a majority of the mass—a majority of the whole people of the Union. If this were so,—if it were true that this is a government of a majority of the whole people, Grover Cleveland would now be President of the United States, instead of Benjamin Harrison, for Cleveland got 100,000 more votes than Harrison. If it were so, Rutherford B. Hayes would not have been President, for there was a majority of more than 300,000 against him in the election of 1876.

If it were so, Abraham Lincoln would not have been President, for nearly a million more votes were cast against him than were cast for him in the election of 1860. If it were so, neither John Quincy Adams, Zachary Taylor, nor James Buchanan would have been President, for Adams had 50,000 less of the popular vote than Jackson; Taylor had 50,000 less than half the popular vote; and Buchanan had 200,000 less than half the popular vote. But it is not so. As little as any other is this a government of a majority of the mass.

This disposes of the Britannica's dictum as to the Constitution, and its teachings as to the nature of our Government, and exposes the fallacy of the saying that this is "a Government of the people, by the people, for the people." The quotations I have given from Davis, Stephens, Henry Lee and Madison, and from the Constitution itself, as well as the whole history of its formation and its daily working, show that this Government was made by States, of States, for States ;—that it is not an empire of provinces, but a federated republic, composed of independent States.[1]

1. In the case of Ware vs. Hilton (3 Dallas, p. 224) the Supreme Court of the United States, Justice Chase delivering the opinion, decided that when the Continental Congress declared the Thirteen United Colonies free and independent States, it was "a declaration, not that the United Colonies, *jointly*, in a collective capacity, were independent States, etc., but that *each* of them was a sovereign and independent State." See Addendum C.

## VI.

With its characteristic dogmatism, and true to the monarchical spirit that pervades it, the Britannica says that Alexander Hamilton was the ablest American jurist and statesman. It is not at all surprising to find in the Britannica such an estimate as that, of the American who called democracy "a disease." Most foreign writers have this opinion of Hamilton, because of his anti-Democratic, monarchical tendencies, but, per contra, Justice Bradley, of the United States Supreme Court, says: "The opinions of Marshall are the standard authority on constitutional questions. In crystalline clearness of thought, irrefragable logic, and a wide and statesmanlike view of all questions of public consequence he has had no superior in this or any other country;" and Alexander H. Stephens, in his writings, says: "Of all the statesmen in this country, none ever excelled Mr. Jefferson in grasp of political ideas, and a thorough understanding of the principles of human government;" and Prof. John Fiske, the accomplished scholar and historian, who has made the history of this Government the subject of his special study, says that Madison "was superior to Hamilton in sobriety and balance of powers," and adds the well known fact that the Government was more Madison's work than that of any other one man.

Here we have the Britannica on one side, and an eminent American jurist, a distinguished American statesman, and a learned American author on the other. Justice Bradley says Hamilton was not an abler jurist than Marshall, Mr. Stephens says he was not an abler statesman than Jefferson, and Prof. Fiske says Madison was his superior in sobriety and balance of powers. Is not this, to say the least of it, calculated to shake somewhat the faith of the Britannica worshipers in the infallibility of their big literary fetish? As to Hamilton, I suspect the truth is that the world will never know how much he is indebted for his reputation to the superior judgment and wise counsel of Philip Schuyler, his father-in-law.

### DID HE "RETIRE WITH DIGNITY"?

When it comes to American history the Britannica seems to have the knack of being found directly opposed by well established facts and the highest American authorities. Take, for instance, the statement in its article on John Adams that "he" (Adams) retired with dignity to his native place," after his defeat in the Presidential election of 1800; whereas the truth is that he retired in a huff—in a very undignified manner—so mad that he didn't stay in Washington to see the inauguration of his successor, with whom he had no intercourse for thirteen years afterward.

### IT GOES WRONG ON "THE FEDERALIST."

In its article on American Literature the Britannica alludes to "The Federalist" as a newspaper—calling it "the organ of the anti-Democratic party;" whereas it is well known to those familiar with American literature that "The Federalist" is the name of a book composed of articles on the Constitution by certain distinguished American statesmen. It is the most famous American political text book, and if the authors of the Britannica had studied it properly they would not have displayed such ignorance as they have in regard to this Government.

### IT BLUNDERS ABOUT JEFFERSON.

In its article on Thomas Jefferson the Britannica says that he was the author of the ordinance passed by Congress for the government of the North-west Territory, containing the provision that there should be no slavery, after the year 1800, in any State organized from that territory. That is what the Britannica says, but the fact is that Thomas Jefferson was not in the United States when that ordinance was passed. He was residing in Paris as minister to the French court at that time (1787), and George Ticknor Curtis, Alexander H. Stephens, and Daniel Webster, and other high American authorities say that Nathan Dane was the author of that ordinance. (See Ticknor's Constitutional History of the United States, vol. I, p. 549; Stephens's War Between the States, vol. I, p. 512; Webster's Works, vol. III, p. 263, 8th ed.) Here again we have the foreign cyclopedia refuted by distinguished American statesmen and historians.

### IT TELLS WHAT "LED TO THE WAR OF '61."

In further reference in the same article to the North-west Territory, the Britannica says: "It was the attempt to organize States from this territory in defiance of this restriction (as to

slavery) that led to the war of 1861." This is the worst yet.
What was called the North-west Territory was the territory between the Ohio and Mississippi rivers, now comprised in the
States of Ohio, Indiana, Illinois, Michigan and Wisconsin—
which, as I have before stated, was ceded to the United
States by Virginia; and it was, according to the Britannica's statement in its article on Jefferson, the attempt to organize these
States in violation of law that led to the war of 1861! This is
even worse than the statement elsewhere in this same encyclopedia that, during that war, the Northern cavalry traversed the
Southern high roads on bicycles and tricycles![1] Really, the Britannica writers should have consulted some of the school-boys and
girls of Montgomery in the preparation of its articles on American
history.

### IT MISREPRESENTS TILDEN.

The Britannica says that Mr. Tilden consented to the creation
of the electoral commission for deciding the disputed result of
the presidential election of 1876. This is another reminder of
the old saying about going from home to learn the news. Nobody on this side of the Atlantic ever heard Mr. Tilden consent
that the result of that election should be determined in any way
not prescribed by the Constitution, but here comes a cyclopedia
from a foreign land three thousand miles away, with the information that he did so consent. Where did the big foreign literary
fetish get its information on this point? The fact is that Mr. Tilden was opposed to having an electoral commission to decide the
result of that election.

### A LESSON IN GEOGRAPHY.

The Britannica says: "The Chattahoochee river is navigable
from Macon to the Gulf of Mexico during the greater part of the
year." (See article on Columbus, Georgia.) Now the fact is that
the Chattahoochee river is not navigable from Macon during the
greater part of the year. The fact is that it is not navigable from

---

1. Commenting on this statement and others of the same character in the Britannica,
the Atlanta Constitution said: "There is something attractive about these bold and
dashing statements. They pique the reader's curiosity. When the stern troopers of
Custer and Kilpatrick trundled along on their bicycles through Virginia and
Georgia it is plain that they must have found a better system of country roads than we
know anything about. This fact alone is sufficiently puzzling, but when we reflect
that bicycles were not in use until several years after the close of the war, the matter
assumes a very interesting aspect. How did the federal cavalry get hold of bicycles
ten years in advance of their fellow-citizens? But we can not pursue the subject. *
* * The description of American military methods is as good as anything that Jules
Verne has ever written."

Macon during any part of the year. Indeed, the fact is that the Chattahoochee river is not at nor near Macon at all. Beyond all question the authors of the Britannica made a very great mistake in not consulting some Alabama or Georgia school-boy or girl in the preparation of its articles touching American history, geography, etc. If they had done so the Britannica would certainly have contained something about Birmingham, Alabama, and an article on Austin, Texas, to say nothing of Brunswick, Georgia.

## "HAMLET" WITHOUT HAMLET.

To write a history of Alabama with no mention of Bienville is like playing Hamlet with the part of Hamlet left out, and yet this is just what the authors of the Britannica have done. The reader of its article on Alabama would never learn from that article that such a man as Bienville—whose name is so closely interwoven with the history of the settlement of this great State—ever lived, nor could the reader find in that cyclopedia any article on Bienville. He would find one, though, on a person by the name of Bilfinger, who appears to have been a privy councillor to a duke or something of the sort some hundred and fifty years ago, and who wrote a treatise entitled "Dilucidationes Philosophicæ, De Deo, Anima Humana Mundo," etc. The Britannica authors evidently didn't think it worth while to give space for an article on Bienville, the brave soldier and explorer, the settler of States and founder of cities; nor of James Blair, the founder, and for fifty years the president of the second college in America, but they didn't intend to get left on Bilfinger—a duke's privy councillor and the writer of a Latin treatise. Never! Perish Bienville; let the founder and guiding genius of the Alma Mater of statesmen and sages sink into oblivion, but live Bilfinger!

## IT GETS THERE ON "AMPHIBIA."

But if the Britannica is short on Alabama—to which it gives only a page and a half, it "gets there" in great shape on "Amphibia," to which it devotes twenty-two pages, from which we glean the very interesting and useful information that "the ganglion of the glossopharyngeal nerve appears to coalesce with that of the vagus;" and that "the vagus or pneumogastric, in the perennibranchiate Amphibia, supplies the second and third branchia, and the cucullaris muscle." It also gives the highly gratifying assur-

ance that "the parietofrontals, nasals, premaxillæ, maxillæ, squa-
mosals, palatines, pterygoids, and parasphenoids, the dentary and
angulo-opercular bones, may be removed without injury to the
chondochranium." As the rest of this extremely entertaining
treatise is in the same limpid and fascinating style that distin-
guishes the foregoing extracts, it would be superfluous to state
that no family should be without the Britannica's article on Amphibia.

AND IT IS SOLID ON ARACHNIDA ,MOLLUSCA, ORTHORHOPHA, ETC.

It is nothing more than fair, too, after all that has been said, to
add that the Encyclopedia Britannica is made up, in very great
part, of articles quite similar to the one on Amphibia.—that is,
similar in respect to the absorbing interest of the themes treated,
the diamond-like lucidity of the language in which they are
couched, and the great practical value—the every-day usefulness
—to so many people of the information they impart. Such, for
instance, are its sixty-eight columns on Crustacea, its fifty-eight
columns on Arachnida, its one hundred and sixty-three columns
on Infinitesimal Calculus, and its long treatises on Mollusca, Orthorhopha, Cyclorhapha, Nematocera, Bibroniæ, Psychodidæ,
etc. And surely there is not one among those who possess the
Britannica who has not read over and over again, and each time
with renewing rapture, its hundred and thirty columns on Ichthyology, abounding with such widely interesting and indispensable
information as this: "In the Teleosteous fishes the spinous column consists of completely ossified amphicœlous vertebræ; its
termination is homocercal. The Polypteroidei have their spinous
column formed by distinct osseous amphicœlous vertebræ; and is
nearly diphycercal." Clearly, nobody should go a-fishing without
the Britannica volume with the article on Ichthyology.

What matters it that this Encyclopedia defames the South?
And totally ignores many of her greatest sons? And makes so
many false statements concerning the history of this country, and
is so lacking generally in American subjects, and so defective in
those it does profess to treat? What. matters all this? Isn't it
solid on England and things English, you know? And on Ichthyology, and the Wave Theory of Light, and Hydromechanics, and
Ambrosius Theodosius Macrobius, and Claudius Namatianus Rutilius—and Bilfinger?

## VII.

Not only is it true that but for the genius, patriotism and valor of Southern men the United States could not have won their independence in the War of the Revolution,—that the bond which afterwards bound the States together in a Federal Union was chiefly the creation of Southern statesmanship,—that the subsequent enlargement of the Union to a size twice as great as its original dimensions was the achievement of Southern statesmanship and valor,—that it was a Southern statesman whose patriotism twice saved it from impending dissolution,—not only are all these things true, but it is also true that without the South's contribution to the Union cause during the war between the States, that cause would have been "the lost cause."

The history of that war shows that many of the bravest and most distinguished soldiers and officers of the Union army and navy were Southern men. The President of the United States during that war was a man of Southern birth and lineage. But for Andrew Johnson, a Southern man, who was Vice-President under Lincoln, Tennessee would have been lost to the Union, and but for Francis P Blair, a Southern man who was a general in the Union army, Missouri would, in all likelihood, have joined the Confederacy.[1] It was General George H. Thomas, of Virginia, who stood like a rock between the Union army and destruction at Chickamauga, and at Chattanooga and Mission Ridge dealt the Confederacy blows from which it never recovered. The same general had previously saved the Union army at Mill Springs and Murfreesboro, and shattered Hood's army to pieces at Nashville. A distinguished Confederate has said that those two Southern

1.  Mr. L. E. Chittenden, who was Register of the United States Treasury during the war between the States, has recently published a book entitled "Recollections of Mr. Lincoln," in which he says that one of the most critical periods in the existence of the Union was the day appointed for the official count of the Presidential vote of 1860, which took place in the presence of both Houses of Congress on February 13, 1861. Mr. Chittenden asserts that this was a moment of imminent danger to the Union, for it was, he says the day appointed for the seizure of Washington and the accomplishment of a revolution by armed bodies of men hostile to the inauguration of Lincoln, and determined upon preventing, in that way, the counting of the vote; and he declares that he believed at the time, and has never since doubted, that the country was indebted for the peaceful count of the electoral vote, for the proclamation of the election of Mr. Lincoln, and for the suppression of the revolution projected for that day, to Major-General Scott and Vice-President Breckenridge. Commenting on this, the New York Sun says: "It is assuredly a curious fact, if fact it be, that two men, both Southern born, should, on Feb. 13, 1861, have carried the republic safely through one of the most imminent perils that ever threatened its existence."

men—Andrew Johnson and George H. Thomas—dug the grave of the Confederacy.

It was General Nelson, a Southern man in the Union army, who first came to Grant's relief at Shiloh, and saved him from destruction there; Newton, a Virginian, commanded the first corps of the Union army at Gettysburg, and was afterwards chief of engineers of the United States army; and we have General Sherman's word for it that "one of the chief causes of Lee's surrender was the skillful, hard march, the night before, of the troops under General Ord," another Southern man in the Union army. The standard work on ordnance in the United States army during the war between the States was by a Southern man—Laidley, of Virginia. Besides those named there were many other distinguished soldiers in the Union army who were Southern men; and its surgeon-general was a Southern man.

Admiral Farragut, the greatest naval commander on the Union side, was a Southern man; so was his fleet-captain and chief-of-staff, his fleet-engineer, and his fleet-surgeon. The commander of his flag ship in the battle of Mobile Bay was a Drayton, of South Carolina; and the ship selected to accompany his flag-ship in that battle was commanded by a Southern man. The blockade vessel that captured more prizes than any other during the war was commanded by a Southerner; a Southerner commanded the monitor that captured the Confederate iron-clad in Warsaw Sound; it was a Southern officer in the United States navy who, at Pensacola, performed what Admiral Porter says was, without doubt, the most gallant cutting-out affair that occurred during the war, and of whom Mr. Greeley makes special complimentary mention in his history, and to whom Mr. Lincoln personally expressed his gratitude;[1] the commander of the iron-clad division of the fleet at the attack on Fort Fisher—to whom, more than to any other officer, was due the capture of that fort—was a Virginian; and a North Carolinian commanded the ship that sunk the Alabama, the famous Confederate vessel commanded by Raphael Semmes.

Finally, there were in the Union armies more than 300,000 men from the Southern or slave-holding States, exclusive of the more than 200,000 negroes who were taken from their Southern owners and mustered into the military service of the Union;—making in all

1. John H. Russell, of Maryland.

more than half a million men the United States Government had
from the South itself with which to fight the Confederacy—largely
more than half the entire number of troops in the Confederate
armies.

Verily, in all truthfulness might it be written of the dead Confederacy,—

" 'Twas thine own genius gave the final blow,
And helped to plant the wound that laid thee low:
So the struck eagle, stretch'd upon the plain,
No more through rolling clouds to soar again.
View'd his own feather on the fatal dart,
And wing'd the shaft that quiver'd in his heart:
Keen were his pangs, but keener far to feel
He nursed the pinion that impell'd the steel."

And now I must take leave of the Encyclopedia Britannica.
An enumeration of all its sins of commission and omission in its
various departments—scientific as well as historical and literary—
would fill a volume of itself and require more time than I have at
my disposal for that purpose.

My object has been chiefly to vindicate the South from its out-
rageous aspersion, and therefore I have not dwelt upon its grave
defects in other directions, prominent among which is the fact that
it contains no notice of any living person. History, without our
contemporaries, is only half history; and it is simply ridiculous to
claim completeness as a cyclopedia for a work that has not biographies of the very men whose deeds, in one form or another,
attract the greatest amount of general attention, but no biographies are to be found in the Britannica of Bismarck, Moltke,
Gladstone, Kossuth, Huxley, Tyndall, Herbert Spencer,
Tennyson, Edwin Arnold, Swinburne, Browning, Castelar,
Carnot, Cleveland, Blaine, or any man or woman now living anywhere in the world. Commenting on this omission of these and
other prominent characters, "The Nation" has aptly said: "To
present history without them is a task which lies well beyond the
abilities of the editor-in-chief and his assistant corps of editors."
A striking instance of this defect was brought to my attention recently by a gentleman who said that when news came of the death
of General Joseph E. Johnston he went to his Britannica to obtain
some particular information about the dead general, and failed to
find there anything about him. As General Johnston didn't die

before the publication of that volume of the Britannica which treats of names beginning with the letter "J," no notice of him is in that cyclopedia. So, there is no article in it on Beaconsfield (D'Israeli), or Carlyle, or Darwin, or George Eliot, or Victor Hugo, or Gambetta, or Garibaldi, or Jules Favre, or George Bancroft, or Jefferson Davis, or Robert Toombs, or Howell Cobb, or Benjamin H. Hill; or the poets,—Timrod, Hayne, Ryan and Lanier. As Margaret J. Preston and James R. Randall—two of America's most gifted poets—are still alive, of course no information at all about them is to be had from the Britannica.

## WHAT HE THOUGHT HE WAS GETTING, AND WHAT HE REALLY DID GET.

Of course the gentleman who failed to find in his Britannica the information he wanted about General Johnston was greatly disappointed, not to say disgusted. He got the Britannica under the impression that he was getting a *complete* cyclopedia—one that was fuller, more thorough, more accurate—one that would tell him more about more things and leave less to be desired in the way of general information than all other cyclopedias combined. The publishers and the agent told him it was that kind of a cyclopedia, and showed him some remarks to the same effect from some English and Northern (probably Massachusetts) papers, and he bought it, and now finds that—instead of having a really useful book of reference, such as is suited to the every-day educational needs of American people—he has a collection of elaborate scientific and technical treatises and discussions, philosophical and metaphysical disquisitions, and abstruse ethical essays, where frequently for entire pages the meaning of no two consecutive lines can be comprehended by the average college graduate, not to say the ordinary reader, and much of which is of no more value to the great mass of readers than a Chinese almanac would be. Strike out its surplusage of long, labored treatises, formulas, and useless and unreadable portions, and the Britannica can be embraced in less than sixteen volumes. For instance, in one of its volumes, which contains 856 pages, 471 of those pages are filled with treatises on nine subjects. Of course this method of construction renders it of little value as a book to be consulted for information about the most of the subjects which are essential to the general reader, and for which a cyclopedia is most frequently and most profitably consulted. Those long treatises do not leave room enough for the subjects in which the great majority of people are most interested.

As the Britannica devotes no space to living people, one would naturally expect to find in it information about more of those who are not living than in cyclopedias that include both. But such is not the case. Other cyclopedias not only tell us of the thinkers and actors who are making history and shaping the destinies of nations and States to-day, but they tell us of a great many more of the world's distinguished dead than the Britannica tells of.

Another instance of its lack of readily accessible information on topics of living interest may be cited in the case of the editor of a leading journal who was expressing his disappointment at not finding in his Britannica any articles on "The Latin Union," the "Monetary Commission of the United States Congress," the "International Monetary Conference," and "Inter State Commerce." The truth is that the Britannica is, properly speaking, only a semi-cyclopedia.

A GLANCE AT ITS EUROPEAN FIELD.

It is not within the purview of this writing to follow the Britannica into other fields than that which I have been specially reviewing; otherwise I should comment on the absence from its pages of biographies of such historic characters as Berthier, Bertrand, Bessières, Brune, Caulaincourt, Cambronne, Davoust, Duroc, Grouchy, Mortier,—those soldiers of the French Republic and of the Empire under the great Napoleon who carried the eagles of France in triumph over so many battle fields and filled the world with the fame of their martial deeds; and the vicomte de Beauharnais, first husband of the empress Josephine; and Cadoudal, whom Bonaparte could not bribe with place or gold; and Bugeaud; and Bouille; and Rochambeau; and Bagration and Kutusow, the great Russian generals; and Biron, the Russian duke and regent whose career was so remarkable and thrilling; and the queens Brunehaut and Fredegonda, whose rivalries constitute a long, bloody and fateful episode in French history; and Bernardo del Carpio; and Catalani; and those world-famous heroines, Grace Darling, Florence Nightingale, and Flora McDonald; and Agnes Bernauer, whose unhappy love and pathetic fate plunged a country into war; and Beatrice Portinari; and Behring, the famous navigator (Behring's strait); and Eric, the Norwegian adventurer; and Praise God Barebones; and Jack Cade; and Blondel, the hero of one of the most exquisitely romantic stories in literature; and Brian Boru (Boroimhe), the Irish hero immortalized in Tom Moore's words—"Remember the glories of Brian the brave." (We couldn't remember them if we depended on the Britannica for the knowledge of them.)

I know it is astounding and almost incredible that, in an Encyclopedia for which so much is claimed as is claimed for the Britannica, there are no articles on the characters here named, but it is a fact, nevertheless; and, after all, is it much stranger than that there is in the same cyclopedia no such title as "Thermopylæ," nor "Borodino," nor "Aspern," nor "Arcola," nor "Campo Formio," nor "Brienne," nor "Balaklava," nor—but I cannot follow it through the European field. Its defects in that field revealed by a cursory glance at the titles under the first few letters of the alphabet sufficiently indicate the proportions to which the list would grow under closer inspection from "A" to "Izzard," and that would involve too wide a departure from the purpose of this writing, which is to vindicate the South from a great aspersion (as I have said), and to show that the book in which that aspersion is published is the last one that an American should get if what he wants is a book from which he can quickly and accurately inform himself on American history and geography, American biography and literature, and, in short, on all those subjects upon which nine hundred and ninety-nine people out of a thousand are most likely to want information in the daily affairs and conversation of life.

WHAT A CYCLOPEDIA SHOULD BE.

A cyclopedia, to fill the measure of the true signification of the term, should be a dictionary of general knowledge, so divided and classified that any desired fact or principle can be found with the greatest practicable facility,—an epitome of the most valuable knowledge, which can be easily consulted, readily understood, and promptly applied, without the toil of picking out a few grains of available gold from a discouraging mass of matter written for exclusively scientific readers, and of the most abstruse scientific character. This is just what the Britannica is not. It is the very reverse of this, and is therefore of comparatively small value to all except masters in special departments of science or art, who

have both the time and the ability to grapple with technical sub-
tleties, obscure terminology, and intricate discussions. Its publishers, though, in offering it for sale to the American people, as-
sured them that it would be "thorough and accurate in the Geography, History, and Institutions of America, and an authorita-
tive book of reference for English-speaking communities in every
quarter of the globe," and upon the strength of this assurance
they sold thousands of copies of the work throughout this country. Do the facts sustain the representation upon which the publishers sold it? Is it thorough and accurate on the Geography,
History, and Institutions of America? If it is not, has not fraud
been practiced, in the selling of it, by those who sold it upon
those who bought it because of their faith in that representation?

### A GREAT IMPOSITION.

The truth is that the sale of the Encyclopædia Britannica to the
American people as the reference-book best suited to their wants
is the greatest imposition, in the book-selling line, ever practiced
upon a people. The low price for which it can now be had and
the attempts at "Americanizing" it are proofs of this truth. Long
before the last volume of the cumbrous work had been delivered
to the thousands who had been induced to subscribe for it, its
worthlessness as a reference book for the people was manifest, and
it had consequently become a drug on the market. Then the
price began to fall, and kept falling till the Britannica could be
had for half its former cost, but its inutility had by this time become still more widely known, and it still remained a drug.
. As a last resort in the strenuous efforts to sell it, in one form or
another, an "Americanized Britannica" is announced, and the
publishers are placing it in the offices of newspapers, to be sold at
*one-fourth* of the original cost of the Britannica, to every one who
will at the same time subscribe for the paper that is selling it !
This is a shrewd device for keeping up a fast falling fabric, for of
course the papers with which this arrangement is made proceed
at once to pronounce it the best of all cyclopedias. It is "strictly
business" with them. Their object is to extend their own circula-
tion, and as long as they can get a subscriber for themselves, and
a handsome commission besides, for every copy of the Britannica
they sell, they will of course "boom" the Britannica. But how
are the mighty fallen! The much-vaunted "monarch of encyclo-

pedias," from a hundred and twenty dollars down to thirty, and a newspaper thrown in! Which is the chromo, the paper or the Britannica?

I have not seen the Britannica in this, its latest guise, but it is presumably the same old English dish, with more American trimmings, but with the same venom in it towards the South,—the same venomous misrepresentation that has made the world at large regard the South as an ignorant, illiterate, semi-barbarous section of the American people, sunk in brutality and vice, that has contributed nothing to the advancement of mankind. If this is the case,—if this misrepresentation of the South is perpetuated in the so-called Americanized Britannica, then the publishers of the papers that are engaged in selling it—for profit to themselves —to the people of this country, should send a copy of this pamphlet along with every copy of the cyclopedia they sell, so that the truth may go along with the falsehood—the antidote with the poison which they are employed in disseminating. This much, at least, is due from them to the people who are traduced by the Britannica, and into whose homes they are placing that work. I would say, however, to those who may be so enamored of the title "Britannica" that they feel that it is not possible for a cyclopedia with any other title to be as good as one which bears that name, that if they will wait a while longer before they buy it they will in all probability (judging from the rate at which it has been falling) be able to get a Britannica at a much lower price than the one at which it is now offered. So rapid has been its depreciation during the last few years that I shall not be surprised to see it going for fifteen or twenty dollars, or less, within the next year or two. But I trust that the days for duping the people of the South into buying the Britannica are over. Shall we continue to buy the literature that slanders us? Other and better cyclopedias are to be had, from sources less ignorant of and less prejudiced against this section than those which inspired the British work, and to them should our preference be given.

ANGLO-MANIACS.

There are, as I have said, some who have been impressed with the belief that in the Britannica they have the ne plus ultra of human knowledge. They read and are imposed upon by its extraordinary claims, gaze upon its big volumes and its pictures, are

deeply struck with its big-sounding title, and its long monographs
(which they will never read and couldn't understand if they were
to read them), and, affected, doubtless, with that mental ailment
pathologically known as Anglo-mania—the subjects of which may
be recognized by the extravagant regard they have for whatever is
"English, you know"—they buy it, set it up, and prostrate themselves before it in an attitude of abject intellectual adoration.
Many of them worship simply its outside—its title, and have
probably never read half a dozen pages in it, and don't know that
they have in their libraries a book which not only maligns the
South, but which also

### MAKES WAR ON THE CHRISTIAN RELIGION

.

to such an extent as to cause the New York *Christian Advocate* to
say,—"The Encyclopædia Britannica is pervaded by a spirit of
prejudice against evangelical Christianity;" and the *Christian In-
telligencer* to say,—"We have been asking ourselves, 'Is this Encyclopædia edited in the interest of modern skepticism?' We are
beginning to ask ourselves also, whether it would not be wise to
request to be released from our subscription to the work, and
whether we might not as well subscribe to a new edition of Paine's
Age of Reason, revised and enlarged by the most eminent skep-
tics of the day;" and the New Orleans *Presbyterian* to say,—"It
is clearly evident that this Encyclopædia is controlled by those
who belong not to the army of the Defenders of the Faith, but to
the host which are studiously seeking to undermine its battlements
and to sap the foundations of the Christian religion." Such is the
Encyclopedia Britannica from the stand-point of the most enlightened Christianity. When its publishers realize that they cannot dupe the people into buying the "Americanized Britannica,"
perhaps they will then try them with a "Christianized Britannica."

### A POISONED FOUNTAIN.

If, in what I have written, I have but partially removed the
film that has hidden from the intellectual vision of any Britannica
worshiper the defects and monstrosities of his literary fetish, I
have done him a service. He should be informed of them, and
he should keep these papers as, in some sort, a refutation of its

falsities and an antidote for its teaching. Especially should every Southern and Christian parent know that, in sending his children to it for information about their native land and the religion of their fathers, he is sending them to a poisoned fountain.

[*From the Montgomery Advertiser, March 22, 1891.*]

# THE LEES OF VIRGINIA,

## "LIGHT-HORSE HARRY" OF THE REVOLUTION, AND HIS IMMORTAL SON.

### There was no Relationship Between Them and the General Lee of the Revolution—Something More About General Charles Lee—History for Northern Writers and Readers.

*To the Editor of the Advertiser:*

In the Advertiser of the 17th inst., you refer to an article going the rounds of the Northern papers headed, "General Lee, of the Revolution—A new discovered manuscript which places him in a bad light—He had a contempt for Washington." Commenting on this you say that the Northern papers publishing the article do not once indicate that there were two Lees who were distinguished officers in the American army during the Revolution—one, General Charles Lee, an Englishman by birth, and an adventurer and a soldier of fortune by profession; the other, Henry Lee, a Virginian by birth, the commander of Lee's legion, the "Light-horse Harry" of the Revolution, the beloved of Washington, and the father of the immortal Robert E. Lee. He it was, as you correctly say, who first called Washington "the man first in war, first in peace, and first in the hearts of his countrymen."

I am not surprised at the Northern papers' not publishing the fact that the Lee referred to in that article was not the father of Robert E. Lee—was not a Virginian—but was Charles Lee, the Englishman. It was this same Gen. Charles Lee who was wounded in a duel by Col. Laurens, of South Carolina, who challenged Lee for language disrespectful to Washington. He was court-martialed and suspended from command for disobedience of orders, misbehavior before the enemy, and disrespect of the commander-in-chief; and was subsequently dismissed from the service for writing an impertinent letter to Congress. Documentary evidence discovered nearly a hundred years afterwards shows that he plotted treason against the American cause. He was the second officer in command in the Revolutionary army, ranking next to Washington. He had high talent and literary culture, but was extremely eccentric, irascible, vain and boastful. His inordinate vanity and thirst for distinction led him to try to create the impression that he was the author of the "Letters of Junius," and he therefore figures in the literature on that subject as one of the many to whom the authorship of those celebrated letters has been attributed, for there were some who, for a time, believed that he really did write them. Investigation showed that there was nothing to sustain the claim for him. The facts disclosed wholly disproved it.

THE USUAL NORTHERNER'S APPALLING IGNORANCE OF AMÉRICAN HISTORY.

There was no relationship between Gen. Charles Lee and the illustrious Virginia family of the same name. I don't suppose that the facts are known to the Northern editors who are publishing the article in question. No doubt they suppose that the General Lee to whom it refers was the Virginian, and the father of Robert E. Lee, notwithstanding the fact that Henry Lee's rank in the Revolution was that of Lieutenant-Colonel, and not General. He did not bear the title of General till he was appointed by President Washington to command the army sent to quell the "Whisky Insurrection" in Pennsylvania, some years after the Revolution. I do not doubt that the Northern editors are wholly unaware of these facts. The density of the usual Northerner's ignorance of the history of his country is something appalling.

"GATH" AND THE BOSTON EDITOR.

A few years ago the most noted of Northern newspaper writers —Mr. George Alfred Townsend, commonly known as "Gath"—in an elaborate historical paper (so-called) in the Boston Globe, said that it was largely through the influence of the writings comprised in the book called "The Federalist" that the convention was called that framed the Constitution of the United States! And the Boston editor called the special attention of his readers to the exceptional historical value of Mr. Townsend's paper, and

announced that it was to be published in book form for the instruction of the New England youths in the history of their
country! Think of such ignorance as that, in the last decade of
the nineteenth century, and in Boston !

And it is only a few months since this same noted writer,
"Gath," in another historical article (so-called), said that "the two
principal writers of the essays called "The Federalist" were John Jay
and Alexander Hamilton ! And yet there are thousands of people
who read almost daily "Gath's" two, three and four column letters, and think, like the Boston editor, that they are getting history in doing it.

### MRS. CLEVELAND'S GOOD EXAMPLE.

Verily, it is high time for the formation of clubs or societies all
over the land for the encouragement of the study of American
history. Mrs. Cleveland and other genuine American women
have started a movement of that kind among the women of New
York, and it is an example that should be followed in every
American city, and town. Especially should the people of the
South welcome and encourage it, for no other section has suffered
as much as it has from the misconception and prejudice resulting
from ignorance of the history of this country, and no other section
has so much of glory to gain from the dissemination of a full and
accurate knowledge of that history.

### HENRY LEE.

Recurring to the Lees, let me say through the Advertiser for
the information of the Northern editors who are exulting in the
belief that they have found something that besmirches the fame
of the father of Robert E Lee, that if they will read page 762 of
the eighth volume of The International Cyclopedia they will find
there these words:

"Henry Lee, a distinguished American general, was one of the
most daring, vigilant and successful cavalry officers on the side
of the colonists. Lee's legion was probably the most effective and
courageous body of troops raised in America. In the famous retreat of Greene before Cornwallis it formed the rear-guard, the
post of honor, and covered itself with glory. At the battles of
Guildford court-house and Eutaw, at the sieges of Forts Watson,
Motte, and Granby and Augusta, and at the storming of Fort
Grierson, Lee particularly signalized himself."

ROBERT E. LEE.

Then if the Northern editors will read further in the same Cyclopedia, they will find there these words:

"Robert E. Lee, son of the preceding, was commander in-chief
of the army of the Confederate States of America.    *    *    *
*    *   He defended Richmond against the Federal army under McClellan and after six days of sanguinary battles drove him
to the shelter of his gunboats. Marching north, he defeated General Pope in the second battle of Manassas. Crossing the Potomac
into Maryland, with a force of 40,000, he was met at Antietam by
McClellan with 80,000, and after a bloody, but indecisive conflict,
recrossed the Potomac and took a position at Fredericksburg,
where he was attacked by General Burnside, whose army he defeated with great slaughter. Gen. Hooker, the successor of Generals McClellan, Pope and Burnside, whom Lee had successively
defeated, crossed the Rappahannock May 1st, 1863, and was attacked by Gen Lee, routed with heavy loss and compelled to
escape in the night across the river." (Some dates are omitted
here for the sake of space.)

On page 767 of the same volume, the Northern editors, if they
will pursue the interesting and truthful line of historical reading
on which I have put them, will find these words: ' Gen. Joseph
Hooker had been appointed to supersede Gen. Burnside, and
with a powerful army now declared his intention to make quick
work of ousting the Confederate army from Fredericksburg. His
army was double in numbers that of Lee. On April 29 he had
massed six army corps on the north side of the Rappahannnock
near Chancellorsville, and should have chosen his own battlefield.
The genius of Lee was never more conspicuous than at this time.
He took the initiative of attack before Hooker's army was through
the 'wilderness,' and detaching Gen. 'Stonewall' Jackson with
21,000 men to make a long circuit to the rear of the right flank of
the Union army, he occupied Gen. Hooker with menaces in front
until the evening of the 30th, when Jackson's attack fell like a
thunderbolt from a clear sky on the rear of the Union army.
The next morning the attack was made real in the front, and such
was the paralysis of the Union commanders, and such was the
mastery of the time and place for action on the part of Lee, that
the great army of Hooker was already defeated.    *    *    * On

May 4th the whole Union army was in full retreat, completely out-
generaled at all points."

"Lee now organized his army to renew the invasion of Pennsylvania.  *  *  *  He maneuvered so as to force Hooker with all
his army to follow, but at the same time so attenuated his line as
to draw the following characteristic letter from President Lincoln
to Gen. Hooker: 'If the head of Lee's army is at Martinsburg
and the tail of it on the plank-road between Fredericksburg and
Chancellorsville, the animal must be very slim somewhere; could
you not break him?' But Hooker was evidently afraid of Lee
anywhere, and with reason." Then follows on the same page an
account of the battle of Gettysburg, closing with these words:
"On the afternoon of the 3rd (July, 1863,) Lee massed 145 cannon
and opened the battle with their thunder, under cover of which
his attacking columns were formed. The attack was all that human
bravery could make it; but the column melted before the fire
that waited for it; and though its head reached and covered the
key of the struggle, the main force of the column was annihilated,
and the position retaken. Gen. Lee's noble equanimity was conspicuous in this defeat in the manner of his meeting the disorgan-
ized remnant of that returning column; infusing them with his
own serene confidence. A retreat was now necessary, but it was
deliberate and orderly, and Gen. Meade, after his victory, found
no place in Lee's army for attack."

THEY SHOULD READ IT ALL.

I am sure the Northern editors must, by this time, be sufficiently
interested in the subject to read the conclusion of the International Cyclopedia's article on Gen. Lee. Aside from the historical instruction they will derive from it, they will find the whole
article a model of clear cut English, well worth perusal for the
chasteness and vigor of its style. Of course only extracts are
given from it here. It concludes as follows:-

"The 'immense campaign' of 1864 for the possession of Richmond was now to test and crown the military fame of Gen. Lee.
Gen. U. S. Grant, victorious thus far on every field, assumed the
personal command of the army of the Potomac. For an entire
year all the vast resources at his command were used with that
rugged grit that regards no loss of life too great which achieves
the quick end of war, and with an energy and skill that all the

world acknowledges. Yet during that entire year Gen. Lee, with an army small in comparison, by his engineering skill, masterly handling, and invariable readiness, held Grant's army at bay, and yielded at last only as a cube of steel may yield to the last great pressure of a colossal vise. Grant was hammering at the front of flint that Lee invariably presented. But the weakening force could but show their heroic valor and the resources of their commander. The last council of war of the army of Northern Virginia was held on the evening of the 8th of April, 1865, and General Lee surrendered the remnant of his troops on the 9th. His parting address to his men is a model of sad dignity and grateful recognition of an army's constancy." * * *

"In person General Lee was of the noblest type of manly beauty; tall, broad-shouldered, erect, with a dignity as impressive as that of Washington, yet not so cold; of habits as pure, more warmly religious; with a calm, confident, kindly manner that no disaster could change. Wishing every one to remain faithful to the old traditions of the South in all that pertained to honor, virtue and hospitality, yet he set himself to work to root up those animosities and provincial rivalries which led only to ruin."

Such were the Lees of Virginia whose names head this article, —Henry Lee, the father; and Robert E. Lee, the son. As they made themselves glorious by their deeds, History has made them glorious by her words, and they

> "Are Freedom's now, and Fame's;
> Among the few, the immortal names,
> That were not born to die."

The South claims them as her own, and proudly says of each of them, as a duke of Ormonde said of an earl of Ossory, "I would not exchange my dead son for any living son in the world." I commend the study of their lives and of our country's history to the millions of uninformed and misinformed people of the North.

T. K. OGLESBY.

Montgomery, Ala., March, 1891.

# ADDENDA.

## ADDENDUM A.

[Referred to on page 13.]

## SHERMAN IN GEORGIA AND CAROLINA.

[Extract from Alexander H. Stephens's History of The War Between the States, Vol. II, pp. 510-511.]

Private houses were sacked, pillaged, and then burnt; and after all family supplies were destroyed, or rendered unfit for use, helpless women and hungry children were left destitute alike of shelter and food. I know men—old men, non-combatants, men who had nothing to do with the war, further than to indulge in that sympathy which nature prompted—who were seized by a licensed soldiery and put to brutal torture, to compel them to disclose and to deliver up treasure that it was supposed they possessed. They were in many instances hung by the neck until life was nearly extinguished, and then cut down with the promise to desist if their demands were complied with, and threats of repeating the operation to death if they were not. Judge Hiram Warner, one of the most upright and unoffending, as well as one of the most distinguished citizens of Georgia, was the victim of an outrage of this sort. He had had nothing to do with the war; but it was supposed he had money, and that was what these "truly loyal" "Union Restorers," so-called, were most eager to secure. Instances of a similar character are numerous and notorious. In some cases, where parties resisted, their lives as well as their purses, watches and other articles of value, were taken!

[The following extracts are from a Pamphlet on The Destruction of Columbia, South Carolina, written and published in 1865, by the gifted and accomplished William Gilmore Simms, LL. D.]

The destruction of Atlanta, the pillaging and burning of other towns of Georgia, and the subsequent devastation along the march of the Federal army through Georgia, gave sufficient earnest of the treatment to be anticipated by South Carolina should the same commander be permitted to make a like progress in our State.

\* \* \* \* \* \*

Half naked people cowered from the winter under bush-tents in the thickets, under the eaves of houses, under the railroad sheds, and in old cars left them along the route. All these repeated the same story of suffering, violence, poverty, and nakedness. Habitation after habitation, village after village—one sending up its signal flames to the other, presaging for it the same fate—lighted the winter and midnight sky with crimson horrors.

\* \* \* \* \* \*

No language can describe nor can any catalogue furnish an adequate detail of the wide-spread destruction of homes and property. Granaries were emptied, and where the grain was not carried off it was strewn to waste under the feet of the cavalry or consigned to the fire which consumed the dwelling. The negroes were robbed equally with the whites of food and clothing. The roads were covered with butchered cattle, hogs, mules, and the costliest furniture. Valuable cabinets, rich pianos, were not only hewn to pieces, but bottles of ink, turpentine, oil, whatever could efface or destroy was employed to defile and ruin. Horses were ridden into the houses. People were forced from their beds to permit the search after hidden treasures.

\* \* \* \* \* \*

Hardly had the troops reached the head of Main street (in Columbia), when the work of pillage was begun. Stores were broken open within the first hour after their arrival, and gold, silver, jewels and liquors eagerly sought. The authorities, officers, soldiers, all, seemed to consider it a matter of course. And woe to him who carried a watch with gold chain pendant; or who wore a choice hat or overcoat, or boots or shoes. He was stripped in the twinkling of an eye. Purses shared the same fate.

\* \* \* \* \* \*

No one felt safe in his own dwelling; and, in the faith that General Sherman would respect the Convent and have it properly guarded, numbers of young ladies were confided to the care of the Mother Superior, and even trunks of clothes and treasures were sent thither, in full confidence that they would find safety. Vain illusions! The Irish Catholic troops, it appears, were not brought into the city at all; were kept on the other side of the river. But a few Catholics were among the corps which occupied the city, and of the conduct of these a favorable account is given. One of them rescued a silver goblet of the church, used as a drinking cup by a soldier, and restored it to the Rev. Dr. O'Connell. This priest, by the way, was severely handled by the soldiers. Such, also, was the fortune of the Rev. Mr. Shand, of Trinity (the Episcopal) church, who sought in vain to save a trunk containing the sacred vessels of his church. It was violently wrested from his keeping, and his struggle to save it only provoked the rougher usage.

\*            \*            \*            \*            \*            \*

In a number of cases the guards provided for the citizens were among the most active plunderers; were quick to betray their trusts, abandon their posts, and bring their comrades in to join in the general pillage. The most dexterous and adroit of these, it is the opinion of most persons, were chiefly Eastern men, or men of immediate Eastern origin.

\*            \*            \*            \*            \*            \*

But the reign of terror did not fairly begin till night. In some instances, where parties complained of the misrule and robbery, their guards said to them, with a chuckle: "This is nothing. Wait till to-night and you'll see h—l."

About dark a body of the soldiers fired the dwellings of Mr. Trenholm, General Wade Hampton, and many others. There were then some twenty fires in full blast in as many different quarters.   \*   \*   \*   The men engaged in this were well prepared with all the appliances essential to their work. They did not need the torch. They carried with them, from house to house, pots and vessels containing combustible liquids, composed probably of phosphorus and other similar agents, turpentine, etc., and, with balls saturated in this liquid, with which they also overspread floors and walls, they conveyed the flames with wonderful rapidity from dwelling to dwelling. Each had his ready box of Lucifer matches, and, with a scrape upon the walls, the flames began to rage. Where houses were closely contiguous a brand from one was the means of conveying destruction to the other. \*  \*  \*  \*
The work went on without impediment and with hourly increase

throughout the night. * * It was a scene for the painter of the terrible. * * * Throughout the whole of it the soldiers continued their search after spoil. The houses were soon gutted of their contents. Hundreds of iron safes, warranted "impenetrable to fire and the burglar," were not "Yankee proof." They were split open and robbed. Jewelry and plate in abundance was found. Men could be seen staggering off with huge waiters, vases, candelabra, to say nothing of cups, goblets, and smaller vessels, all of solid silver. Clothes and shoes, when new, were appropriated—the rest left to burn.

*      *      *      *      *      *

Ladies were hustled from their chambers—their ornaments plucked from their persons, their bundles from their hands. It was in vain that the mother appealed for the garments of her children. They were torn from her grasp and hurled into the flames. The young girl striving to save a single frock, had it rent to fibres in her grasp. Men and women bearing off their trunks were seized, despoiled, in a moment the trunk burst asunder, with the stroke of axe or gun butt, the contents laid bare, rifled of all the objects of desire, and the residue sacrificed to the fire.

*      *      *      *      *      *

"Your watch!" "Your money!" was the demand. Frequently no demand was made. Rarely, indeed, was a word spoken, where the watch or chain, or ring or bracelet, presented itself conspicuously to the eye. It was incontinently plucked away from the neck, breast or bosom. Hundreds of women, still greater numbers of old men, were thus despoiled. The venerable Mr. Alfred Huger was thus robbed in the chamber and presence of his family, and in the eye of an almost dying wife. He offered resistance, and was collared and dispossessed by violence. We are told that the venerable Ex-Senator Colonel Arthur P. Hayne was treated even more roughly.

*      *      *      *      *      *

The pistol to the bosom or head of woman, the patient mother, the trembling daughter, was the ordinary introduction to the demand: "Your gold, silver, watch, jewels!" They gave no time, allowed no pause or hesitation. It was in vain that the woman offered her keys, or proceeded to open drawer or wardrobe, or cabinet or trunk. It was dashed to pieces by axe or gun butt, with the cry, "We have a shorter way than that!" It was in vain that she pleaded to spare her furniture, and she would give up all its contents. All the precious things of a family; such as the heart loves to pore on in quiet hours when alone with memory —the dear miniature, the photograph, the portrait—these were dashed to pieces, crushed under foot, and the more the trembler pleaded for the object so precious, the more violent the rage which destroyed it. Nothing was sacred in their eyes save the gold and silver which they bore away. Nor were these acts those of common soldiers. Commissioned officers, of rank so high as that of colonel, were frequently among the most active in spoliation, and, after glutting themselves with spoil, would often utter the foulest speeches, coupled with oaths as condiment.

\*  \*  \*  \*  \*  \*

There are some horrors which the historian dare not pursue— which the painter dare not delineate. They both drop the curtain over crimes which humanity bleeds to contemplate. * * * A lady, undergoing the pains of labor, had to be borne out on a mattress into the open air, to escape the fire. It was in vain that her situation was described as the soldiers applied the torch within and without the house, after they had penetrated every chamber and robbed them of all that was either valuable or portable. They beheld the situation of the sufferer, and laughed to scorn the prayer for her safety.

Another lady, Mrs. J——, was but recently confined. Her condition was very helpless. Her life hung upon a hair. The men were apprised of all the facts in the case. They burst into the chamber—took the rings from the lady's fingers—plucked the watch from beneath her pillow, and so overwhelmed her with terror, that she sunk under the treatment—surviving their departure but a day or two. In several instances, parlors, articles of crockery, and even beds, were used by the soldiers as if they were water-closets. In one case, a party used vessels in this way, then put them on the bed, fired at and smashed them to pieces, emptying the filthy contents over the bedding. In several cases, newly made graves were opened, the coffins taken out, broken open, in search of buried treasure, and the corpses left exposed. Every spot in graveyard or garden, which seemed to have been recently dis-

turbed, was sounded with sword, or bayonet, or ramrod, in their
desperate search after spoil.

---

## JEFFERSON DAVIS'S REGIMENT IN MEXICO.

[Extract from the New York Sun's Review of the Memoir of Jefferson Davis, by his
wife.]

It was a fact well worth recording in this memoir that this regi-
ment, from the Colonel down to the last private, returned home
without a single article belonging to a citizen of Mexico. "The
sacred silver and gold vessels and the church vestments studded
over with precious stones were in an open room at Monterey and
also at Saltillo. The image of the Virgin of Guadalupe, a large
doll dressed in satin, was admired and examined, but left untouched,
though the frock in which she was arrayed was worked in arabesques
adorned with diamonds, rubies, and emeralds of great price,
and she wore a necklace of immense pearls which were of several
colors. Col. Davis saw one of the soldiers, in friendly conversation with an old priest, holding admiringly a gold reliquary, the
top of which was rayed with diamonds, several hundred, he
thought, altogether. The Mexicans felt and had perfect security
for their property."

# ADDENDUM B.

[Referred to on page 18.]

## INTOLERANCE IN MASSACHUSETTS.

The reprehensible and un-American principle of political and religious intolerance has ever found congenial soil in Massachusetts. The spirit of the fathers there descended to the sons, and accordingly we find the notorious Hartford Convention (dominated by Massachusetts men) insisting that the Federal Constitution be amended so that no person naturalized thereafter could be eligible as a member of the Senate or House of Representatives of the United States, nor capable of holding any civil office under the authority of the United States; and forty years later (1855), having failed to get that proscriptive principle into the organic law of the Federal government, the people of Massachusetts then declared not only that no man born outside of the United States should hold office in that State, but "that no man who worshiped God in a Catholic church should hold office in the State." In this connection I think it well worth while to insert an extract from the speech of Hon. James B. Eustis, of Louisiana, in the United States Senate, January 21, 1891. In the course of his powerful speech on that occasion, Mr. Eustis said:

"I would remind the Senator from Massachusetts that, in my estimation and in my judgment, the case of the most relentless, unblushing, cruel, and unconstitutional political proscription is one that occurred in the State of Massachusetts.

"Sir, it was the aim of our fathers who framed the Constitution of the United States that this question of religion should never enter into our political deliberations or political action. From the bloody history of England they gathered the wisdom to provide that the people of the United States should be exempt from that terrible curse, religious contention and religious proscription; that it would be in violation of the spirit of the Constitution that any State or any political party should establish a religious test as a qualification for office in this country.

"And yet, Mr President, do we not remember the period of 1854 and 1855 in the State of Massachusetts, when her people decided by an overwhelming majority, on a question that stirred the State from top to bottom, the principle and the proclaimed determination that no man who worshiped God in a Catholic church should hold office in the State; that before he became qualified (in the estimation of the people of that State), before he could reinstate himself as eligible to political office, no matter how insignificant, in the State of Massachusetts, he must renounce the religion of his mother and bow down to Massachusetts' Protestantism, and worship that God, and that God alone?

"Was that the justice, Mr. President, which the Senator from Massachusetts invokes from us? Was that the toleration which he invokes from us? Ah, Mr. President, if that platform of Massachusetts and that political faith of Massachusetts had not been destroyed and exterminated in this country by the sturdy democracy of this land, this country from one end to the other would have been plunged into civil strife and human blood would have flowed on every political field of this vast domain.

"But this is not all, Mr. President. Not satisfied with making war upon the religion of their fellow-citizens, reviving the days when they burned convents and expelled nuns from their consecrated habitations; not yet satiated with that infernal spirit of political proscription which makes the blackest page that has been written in the history of this country; not satisfied with having gorged themselves with political power secured by having trampled upon the religion of their fellow-citizens, they extended their political warfare and their political proscription in still another direction, and declared in their platform and in their political creed that no man who was born abroad, although he might be a naturalized citizen of the United States, was qualified to hold office in the State of Massachusetts; that Mr. Pat Collins, who has served his State with distinction in the other House; who has conferred—though he would not say so himself—honor upon the constituency which he represented in the other House, and who only a few days ago was tendered a position by a Democratic governor as judge of the supreme court of Massachusetts; that John Boyle O'Reilly, that great Irishman who made fame by his honesty, his patriotism, and his literary attainments, around whose tomb the other day were gathered, irrespective of party, thousands and thousands of Boston's citizens, feeling that the State of Massachusetts had suffered a terrible bereavement—that those two men, under the political creed which existed, and which probably the Senator from Massachusetts, if he had been old enough, would have indorsed, were unworthy for a double reason to hold any office in the State of Massachusetts—one because they were Catholics, and the other because they were foreign-born citizens."

# ADDENDUM C.

[Referred to on page 28.]

## THE FEDERATIVE PRINCIPLE OF OUR GOVERNMENT.

[Alexander H Stephens, in "The War Between the States," Vol. 1, pp. 534-535.]

In the Federative principle of our Government its chief strength, its great beauty, its complete symmetry, its ultimate harmony, and, indeed, its very perfection, mainly consist; certainly, so long as the objects aimed at in its formation are the objects aimed at in its administration. And, on this principle, on the full recognition of the absolute ultimate Sovereignty of the several States, I did consider it the best, and the strongest, and the grandest Government on earth! My whole heart and soul were devoted to the Constitution, and the Union under it, with this understanding of its nature, character, objects, and functions!

When, therefore, the State of Georgia seceded, against my judgment, viewing the measure in the light of *policy*, only, and not of right, I felt it to be my duty to go with her, not only from a sense of the obligations of allegiance, but from other high considerations of patriotism of not much less weight and influence. These considerations pressed upon the mind the importance of maintaining this principle, which lies at the foundation of all Federal systems; and to which we were mainly indebted, in ours, for all the great achievements of the past. It was under this construction of the nature of our system that all these achievements had been attained. This was the essential and vital principle of the system, to which I was so thoroughly devoted. It was that which secured all the advantages of Confederation without the risk of Centralism and Absolutism; and on its preservation depended, not only the safety and welfare, and even existence, of my own State, but the safety, welfare, and ultimate existence of all the other States of the Union! The States were older than the Union! They made it. It was their own creation! Their preservation was of infinitely more importance than its continuance! The Union might cease to exist, and yet the States continue to exist, as before! Not so with the Union, in case of the destruction or annihilation of the States! With their extinction, the Union necessarily becomes extinct also! They may survive it, and form another, more perfect, if the lapse of time and changes of events show it to be necessary, for the same objects had in view when it was form d; but it can never survive them! What may be called a Union may spring from the common ruins, but it would not be the Union of the Constitution!—the Union of States! By whatever name it might be called, whether Union, Nation, Kingdom, or anything else, according to the taste of its dupes or its devotees, it would, in reality, be nothing but that deformed and hideous Monster which rises from the decomposing elements of dead States, the world over, and which is well known by the friends of Constitutional Liberty, everywhere, as the Demon of Centralism, Absolutism, Despotism! This is the necessary reality of that result, whether the Imperial Powers be seized and wielded by the hands of many, of few, or of one!

www.ingramcontent.com/pod-product-compliance
Lightning Source LLC
Chambersburg PA
CBHW031748090426
42739CB00008B/925